WARDROBE OF SELVES

By the same author:

Thunder Road, Thunder Heart
In the Human Night
The Neon Hunger
The Heart at 3 a.m.
Days That We Couldn't Rehearse
Beneath Our Armour
Personal Weather
Le cœur à trois heures du matin
The Elsewhere Variations (with Ken Bolton)

WARDROBE OF SELVES

PETER BAKOWSKI

RECENT
WORK
PRESS

Wardrobe of Selves
Recent Work Press
Canberra, Australia

Copyright © Peter Bakowski, 2019

ISBN: 9780648685302 (paperback)

A catalogue record for this book is available from the National Library of Australia

All rights reserved. This book is copyright. Except for private study, research, criticism or reviews as permitted under the Copyright Act, no part of this book may be reproduced, stored in a retrieval system, or transmitted in any form by any means without prior written permission. Enquiries should be addressed to the publisher.

Cover image and author photograph © Ophelia Bakowski. 2019
www.opheliabakowski.com

Cover design: Ophelia Bakowski with Recent Work Press
Set by Recent Work Press

recentworkpress.com

For Helen and Ophelia Bakowski

Contents

Views from a park bench, the Treasury Gardens, Melbourne, 25 May 2018	1
A sparrow in the Melbourne city library	2
The Magdalen laundries, Abbotsford Convent, Melbourne 1932	3
Homeless man during morning rush hour, Bourke Street	4
Portrait of Emma Palandra in the CBD, Melbourne, July 2018	5
The letter X	6
Paranoia in the English language	6
Misheard	7
Quiet please	7
A sonnet for New Zealand poet, James Brown	8
Magnetic city	9
Wake up call	10
A Skopelos afternoon, July 1962	11
Goat cull on Iura, the Sporades, May 1969	12
Isolated cottage, Skopelos, 16 October 1972	13
Man Ray in his studio, 31 bis rue Campagne-Première, Paris, December 1930	14
The making of agent 12, Paris, December 1942	15
Mr Greene attends a party, Cannes, 19 April 1946	17
A poem addressed to Death	18
Paris days	19
Portrait of a clothes maker	20
Poem to the artists	20
Portrait of Willem de Kooning, Springs, Long Island, 31 December 1973	21
Humanity	23
Andris visits the derelict schoolhouse at Lādes	25
Norillag Labour Camp, Krasnoyarsk Krai, Russia, March 1943	27
Poem to the pebble	28
Fairness reconsidered	29
Wardrobe of selves	30
Intentions	31
First date	31

Winter	32
Poem to the ceiling of Room 6, The Railroad Hotel, Dallas	33
No forwarding address	35
Never to entwine	35
Tiltmouth Tompkins talks to a blues enthusiast, Washington Square Park, 15 October 1959	36
The tipping point	39
Pending their divorce	39
Distribution	40
Heated	40
Some observations and suggestions	41
Self-portrait, lying on the bed, Skopelos, 26 September 2018	42
Island bus ride, Skopelos	43
Tourist couple	44
Bomb blast	44
The end of the season, Skopelos	45
Portrait of Lester Gambell, musician and songwriter, Milledgeville, Georgia, 10 July 1969	46
Proverbs for the 21st century	50
Poem for Ed Ruscha	51
Portrait of a hypochondriac	52
At my craft	53
Observations in the year 2019	55
Portrait of an adulterer	56
Memorandum	57

Views from a park bench, the Treasury Gardens, Melbourne, 25 May 2018

Please rest even recuperate on my slatted lap.
Accept that you may be judged by passersby,
Relegated to a type, perhaps of fanciful vocation—
Kilt-maker, embalmer, lion tamer.

Bustling is for others. Let them stampede to water cooler and
Elevator, while you, in looser clothing, study the plumage of a duck
Nibbling at bread scraps lodged in tufts of grass. You've gravitated,
Chosen to venture here, to undertake this escape or close examination of
How you are or how you aren't, as the autumn leaves loosen and fall.

A sparrow in the Melbourne city library

You're a winged comma in this literate room.
Some of the patrons—students whose reading
is dutiful, each sentence gristle or chore,
are quietly glad of your flitting
which reddens the library assistant's traffic light face
as he puffs and flounders with his net extended.

For long minutes you accept
being less colourful
than the book covers you're circling,
but finding this internal sky
breezeless, tame,
you allow the net its mesh victory—
which brings a halt to your insurrection.

The library assistant, his forehead
no longer such a ploughed field,
exits with you,
both temporarily subdued,
out into Flinders Lane.

Released, you rise and rise—
leave us
to return to our worship
of page and laptop screen.

The Magdalen laundries, Abbotsford Convent, Melbourne 1932

Emerge from stone cold rooms. The penance of work will cure you of
Nocturnal sobbing. Do not voice the
Doubt—that morning prayers may not salve your deepest wounds.
Unending torrent of laundry to starch, iron and fold. Hands are
Raw which once played the piano, dared to hold the hips of a man in
Errant embrace. You must quell the fires of the flesh to be truly saved.

Homeless man during morning rush hour, Bourke Street

Some park bench sleep. Elbow for a pillow.
Half a cigarette for breakfast.
Ask the office-bound for money. Their brisk shoes
grant them safe distance from my pavement cap.
Only a little blood when I cough
into a paper napkin the wind hands me.
Once upon a time I carved a girl's initials and mine
into the trunk of a birch tree.
I look for her
in the swarm of passing faces.

Portrait of Emma Palandra in the CBD, Melbourne, July 2018

Wearing a fake fur,
her greying hair unwashed,
a T2 bag at her feet,
Emma sits in Self Preservation,
hunched over her iPhone.
She's still thinking of phoning Eric
now that the bruise below her left eye has faded.

Eric had insisted things will be better
once he got his hands on a gun—
claimed that he's cased the Lennox Street milk bar
every day for the last month—
the till's a honeypot,
will bankroll them to Noosa.

But Eric has always been
more puff than progress,
more skateboard than limousine.

Feeling sorry for oneself—
Emma has had years of practice.
She walks through the Treasury Gardens,
sits on a park bench,
tells herself that she's worth more
than any scavenging pigeon,
will win more from this world
than crumbs and flight.

The letter X

is cross
with itself.

Paranoia in the English language

Many consonants believe they're being followed by a vowel.

Misheard

After his parents' lecture
Eric did try
to butter himself.

Quiet please

If the walls could talk there'd be
more ear plugs sold.

A sonnet for New Zealand poet, James Brown

Perhaps the man, standing patient at the bus stop, with suede
elbow patches on his jacket, is a humorous poet or a taxidermist.
You can't judge a bed by its doona.

It's considered poetry to find that indeed you have a spare light bulb
in the kitchen cupboard, when it's raining chickens and horses
and the all-night supermarket is first on the left after Alpha Centauri.

You've been left in the dark before and you're been right in the dark
before. Your ambition is to write a poem that will last longer than a
$29 toaster from Coles.

Bruce Springsteen used to be young. He had muscles where some of
us mainly have mucus. Clearly he was born to run rather than jog.
We've plenty of slam poets in Australia, but not enough tiptoe poets.
You clearly recognise that poetry is a raft. Keep fashioning that sail
and mast.

Magnetic city

The girl who hand-rolls thin cigarettes,
the girl with the silver nose ring,
the girl with Mormon parents,
the girl who visits Marlene Dietrich's grave.

The girl who has dyed her hair green,
the girl who used to self-harm,
the girl who realises that she's attracted to women,
the girl who loves and hates her mother.

The girl who was a volleyball captain,
the girl who is learning African drumming,
the girl whose brother drowned,
the girl whose hero is Patti Smith;

may be found in Berlin—
here for Spring break,
for summer vacation,
for the rest of their lives.

Wake up call

Doing can take a lot of doing—
Involves getting off the couch of your thinking.
Find a way out of the fog of your pyjamas. Get vertical.
Flex an eyelid. The sky's still there, the horizon its trump card.
Interest yourself in more than yourself, there are other
Curious beings, relentless in understanding, undressing the
Universe. Look at who you are as a seed not a sentence.
Learn and unlearn. Excuses are more scaffold than building.
Truth—coax it from the hiding place on the tip of your tongue.

A Skopelos afternoon, July 1962

Nikos the postman is asleep near the harbour wall.
No letter is urgent now that the self-important have telephones.

In his leather bag—undelivered postcards he'll keep, a sketchpad
and a much-chewed pencil with which Nikos may sketch
a precarious hillside house made of donkey-hauled stone,
where, seated in tender view of her vegetable patch
of zucchini and bright red peppers,
a widow mends the skirt she often wears
when out gathering sage.

Goat cull on Iura, the Sporades, May 1969

Guns and men board. The skinner sharpens his knives. A flask
Of ouzo is passed around before landfall.
A kill of twenty-five has been sanctioned by officials at Volos.
The hunters scan the crags. Branch out and climb. While

Chewing thistles the first ram is shot, carried through the
Undergrowth on lethal shoulders, to thud on salty canvas that's been
Laid out on the boat deck. Horns and hooves are removed, the
Liver thrown into a rusty bucket.

Isolated cottage, Skopelos, 16 October 1972

Ink spilt on the best tablecloth.
Now that the guests have gone Papa removes his belt, screams

That I deserve such a thrashing.
Healing—never found in the loose-hinged medicine cabinet.
Each cut, each plea, each fleck of blood on the bedroom wallpaper

Prepares me for what I must thieve from this
Implosive house.
Now this dawning hour I'll pay, with
Every drachma stolen, for passage to the mainland where I'll
Sing in concert and dancehall louder than the roar of any father.

Man Ray in his studio, 31 bis rue Campagne-Première, Paris, December 1930

In the developing tray,
hallowed pool of black and white magic,
your body is illuminated, recast.

Your feasting lips float
beyond the tyranny of my stare
to the watering holes of the monied herd.
You soiled grand rooms with gin and nicotine.

I became a burnt moth.
My seared body
thudding against the window panes,
impotent percussion.

But I've re-emerged from the husk of myself,
raise the camera to my gleaning eye.

The next photograph and the thousand after that
are what concern and hardly concern me.

I work my camera,
seek nourishment, nectar—
the blackest flower,
the whitest flower,
the flower that's a drug,
the flower that makes me briefly a flower
as I stand naked in this studio,
flipping a gold coin
with your all-seeing eye
embossed on each side.

The making of agent 12, Paris, December 1942

The river Seine. Each arched bridge is a raised eyebrow.
I put a match to your coded letter.
Burnt embers fall from my releasing hand.

I'm thankful for the hour's walk to my room.

Car headlights scrape at the ceiling
but the water stains are no longer there—
they've scuttled down the walls,
entered my veins.

Your blue handkerchief still serves its purpose,
plugs the mousehole in the bedroom skirting board.
Some faltering nights
I think of jamming that handkerchief into my mouth
which longs to utter your name.

Perhaps you're hiding
in a barn on the outskirts
of some flyspeck village.
Perhaps my identity papers
will incur sharper scrutiny.

Uncertainty. Radio broadcasts and sermons.
I believe in bullets more than words.

These are the heightened hours
of watching, listening,
passing on information.

I wasn't made for this
but I do this.
Crouch behind wine crates
in a piss stench alley,
squeeze the trigger.

The target falls.
I check for a pulse.
There's none.

Sweating,
I slow my walking pace,
head down Rue des Pyrenees,
the stolen Luger
heavy in my handbag.

.

Mr Greene attends a party, Cannes, 19 April 1946

Boldness—you've always admired it in others. The way they
Enter and navigate a room, appear nourished rather than
Numbed by each handshake and kiss, how easily they
Elicit laughter from a crescent of matrons.
Delicately they inquire about the health of your parents, your
Investments and plans for the summer.
Chuffed that they have graced your table, you
Toast their back as they swan onto the dancefloor, now
Invaded by the adulterous and the athletic.
Overcoat retrieved, you exit via the kitchen, the
Night air refreshing memories of when Daphne was still alive.

A poem addressed to Death

Delay your foreclosure on my body. I've some expectations and
Excuses I haven't finished with yet. Many shrug, say that
Accidents will happen—let me give you their likely addresses.
Tarry in cemeteries you've filled. Pat yourself on the skeleton.
How hard you've worked. Take a holiday, an eternity perhaps.

Paris days

Pause. Let a café be a comma in your ambling.
An aperitif may help you digest or digress, decide to turn
Right or left at the intersection of two thoughts.
In essay and sculpture, pursue your questions about our bodies and
Spirit. The gleaning eye is led to mirror, canvas, storied window,

Descends a spiral staircase to witness the birth of a poem. Let
Astonishment not apathy be our daily bread. In the blink of
Years, there remains wariness, restraint in
Stating anything as final. Each arched bridge is a raised eyebrow.

Portrait of a clothes maker

for Édouard Vuillard

Bless this ordered room where Helen threads her
Exacting needle through embroidered cloth,
Altering a summer dress this sunlit hour.
Utter devotion to a craft reveals
The doubt and self-belief in a person. May the incomplete
Yield to discerning eye and hand.

Poem to the artists

Brushstrokes—to reveal the nuances of a person, a room, an
Epoch. What stirs in a face, in the crevice of a wound, is rendered.
Art began on the cave wall. A primal vocabulary. There is a need to
Utter, to forge into being, what wakes the eye, heart and conscience.
This is our glory, our human answer to time, its glacial force. May
Your art impel us to dive deep, beneath the surface of every question.

Portrait of Willem de Kooning, Springs, Long Island, 31 December 1973

King of bluntness,
I paint those in my circle—
all the wounded and wounding,
their cigarette mouths,
sewerage hair.

I pace back and forth,
here in the studio,
pause to toast with another whisky,
my imaginary brother.
From the mirror
he offers no protest
as I sway before
an overworked semblance of myself
which I may wrench from the easel,
stomp underfoot.

I have no steady compass or companion
only these brushstrokes—
yellow, blue, red flares
that I launch into the sky.

Paint fumes and fuming—
Sometimes I fall to my knees exhausted.

I'm looking for the door in each painting,
one that leads beyond the battlefield of my life,
where I can sit in a chair
and think about light,
the way it anoints a bared shoulder,
the paint-peeled hull of a beached dinghy.

I paint
out of knowing
and out of not knowing enough
each granted day and night
until the brush falls
from my striving hand.

Humanity

for Ai Weiwei

Here are the people,
some questioning, some questioned,
some imprisoned, some self-imprisoned.

Here are the people,
model citizens, scapegoats
and those under surveillance while hiking
around the circumference of a lake.

Here are the people,
working, warring, dying
for the self-appointed puppet-makers.
Take a bow, take a truncheon blow
to your straw and newspaper head.

Here are the people,
falling from favour,
falling from high rise building sites,
into infirmaries,
into their death beds,
into the ground,
into statistics,
into dossiers
signed and countersigned,
correctly filed in a room
which only the authorised may enter.

Here are the people,
realising the way things work,
realising the way things don't work.
Some will be angered enough
to speak, to act, to sabotage and subvert.

Their numbers will swell,
topple statues, the bloated regime.

The historians will study the costs,
the toll on the nation.
It may be easier to clear the rubble than one's conscience
and the people will gather in the market squares again
to see what can be bargained, who has survived.

Andris visits the derelict schoolhouse at Lādes

When there were lessons here, I daydreamed—
imagined Latvia as a far-flung island,
never invaded, never occupied—
Russian and German words and commands
never soiling my ears and mouth.

But history wasn't a daydream—
it was the trading of grandmother's pearl earrings
for a brick of bread.
Boiled weeds and thorns in a dented tin cup
became our only soup.
Those moving through the knee-high grass
weren't hunting wolves.
I prayed for the partisans in the forest,
that they weren't betrayed
by a wisp of campfire smoke,
or the full moon.

I've forgotten algebra and physics lessons endured,
but never the two bullets
dug out of my right leg
with a whittling knife
while I bit down on a whisky-soaked rag
in a hayloft less than a kilometre from here.

To kill or be killed
isn't a line of poetry—
it was an order barked by an appointed leader of farmers
armed with pitchforks, axes, knives, shovels, rabbit traps,
and a dozen assorted rifles stolen from the local museum.

Now I'm a shuffle of bones and blood,
angry at nations and the notion of nations—
over the years I've been told so many lies

in speeches, in pamphlets and on bulletin boards.
Now I only believe in nature,
a tuft of grass growing out of a tree stump.

Let me bear witness to the air dance of butterflies.
Let me lay down, sun-caressed, in a field of yellow dandelions.
Let me shed tears for who I have lost.
Let winter come, freeze all the scarring questions
which I cannot answer.

Norillag Labour Camp, Krasnoyarsk Krai, Russia, March 1943

Night. There are more lice than stars.
Hunger—untamed by
strands of cabbage in watery soup,
a knuckle of bread.
Your body's a pauper's sack—nothing in it except
blood-clot coughs, a crumpled map to the precipice of a fever.

Mercy exists, bestowed by the snow, the electrified fence,
the guards' efficient bullets.

Poem to the pebble

Sometimes you strain
to cast a grander shadow—
envy each strutting pigeon.

Let others hunt and slaughter,
puff out their chests,
stain history books.

I suggest you stay
undemonstrative,
grounded,
perhaps only noticed when
you lodge
in our shoes.

Fairness reconsidered

Perhaps you were guided or sternly led
to a sense of obligation when young—given tasks, chores, duties.

Perhaps you slunk away from these or tackled them with vigour.
Consider how you felt at the time about those who commanded,
governed you. Consider your behaviour—whether you honoured
expectations, the trust placed in you, whether those expectations were
reasonable or outrageous.

In our beginning came the cultivation of crops,
our nourishment dependent on toil and knowledge.
Generosity leads to generation. Chances are seeds.
Sometimes the soil must be prodded, turned, aerated, analysed.

Invite dialogue and debate. Let listening be part of your growth.
Let each participating voice be openly heard before
decisions are made. There's no guarantee that everyone'll be satisfied
but the attempt will have been made
and that's honourable, may lead to a handshake, new ways forward.

Wardrobe of selves

Addressing your life. Perhaps that's overdue or not really you

Winking or wilting in front of the mirror. Maybe everything's
Arranged or in disarray. Consider what to wear, what wears you.
Roll with the punches, not with the paunch you may have acquired.
Dressed to the nines or only the fours, perhaps it's time to
Ride that bucking bronco tethered beneath your ribs. Your
Obituary needn't be an ode to daring but if you're able, do venture
Beyond the perimeter of your toenails. Rush or gingerly
Ease into revealing yourself. Who you are may be

Of less importance than how you are—
Flummoxed or fulfilled. Both are cyclical.

Some selves are secret, take themselves to the grave—their
Existence exposed in a diary, a bundle of letters—angers and
Loves, visions and regrets—not torn in half, not rewritten.
Versions of ourselves, face half in shadow under a hat brim,
Elude conclusive portraiture. Brush the lint from your cautious
Shoulders. Your true self may be in the vicinity awaiting your arrival.

Intentions

Ingrid imagines
the book she's yet to write,
there, among the books
she's yet to read.

First date

Hanging in the wardrobe,
the dress Moira would like to wear
next to the one she will.

Winter

When it attacks from the sky of your mind,
Intent on the prey in your mirror,
None but the most willed of pilgrims shall
Travel onwards in such eroding weather, to crush
Each parasitic cloud, free the reefed hull of the sun,
Render the horizon valuable again.

Poem to the ceiling of Room 6, The Railroad Hotel, Dallas

You keep your distance,
don't judge those beneath you,
allow light globe and spider
their dangling.

Gazing at your replastered wounds,
I fabricate stories—

a suicide's first bullet,
misfired by a trembling hand.

the nailing of a full-length crucifix
above a preacher's bed.

Now I watch Bessie the chambermaid
armed with her righteous feather duster
climb a stepladder
to brush away cobwebs from your corners.

Stretching too far
she falls from the ladder onto the floor.

I offer Bessie the flask of whisky
I keep under my bed pillow.

After the second swig,
good colour comes back into Bessie's face.

I grab my National guitar,
sing her my new song
while Bessie has a third and fourth swig of whisky.

I loosen my necktie.
Bessie removes her shoes and apron,
eases her body onto the bed.

Soon enough I'm kissing Bessie's navel,
all her valleys and crests.
Outside a freight train shudders past.
Then for a while
Bessie and me
find the world less meagre
as through the room's only window
the evening's first stream of car headlights
illuminate you.

No forwarding address

The snails in the mailbox
eat away more of Emily's signature
on the uncollected postcard.

Never to entwine

A lone worm in the summer grass
fails to revive the strand of spaghetti
that's fallen from Cynthia's plate.

Tiltmouth Tompkins talks to a blues enthusiast, Washington Square Park, 15 October 1959

for Hari Kunzru

Lipetti the knife thrower taught me guitar,
how to pick and strum,
bend and hold a note,
release a run
that could win an ear,
stop a car.

One night I quit the circus
and kept walking.
Sometimes
farmers let me sleep in their barns,
sometimes religious folk
gave me a bed,
prayed for me and all our tainted souls,
before a breakfast
of ham and eggs.

In southern Illinois,
I stole for the first time—
a pair of muddy shoes from a porch,
a sweater drying on a clothesline.
I'd only seen snow in picture books.

In a soup kitchen
a solid guy
made of bricks and sweat
noticed me,
the battered guitar case at my feet,
indicated with sign language
to follow him.

Block after block
of busted streetlights,
burnt-out storefronts,
then a warehouse door.

Waded into cigarette smoke and sound.
Drums, harmonica
and a 300 pounds singer on his knees,
singing about
blood on a pair of hands,
trying to figure
his next move.

Blues music—
it's a spell and a warning.

House parties.
An upturned hat
filling with cash.
A woman or a man
in the audience,
ready to take you
to heaven or the cleaners.

I became an all the time drunk.
I'd spent 25 years
trying to distance myself
from my pa being lynched—
accused of eyeballing a white woman
when she was doing her Saturday morning
grocery shopping.

My pa eyeballed the family bible
more than he would any stranger
At gigs I'd become a liability,
out of tune with the vertical,
lost in the dark hallway of a song,
groping for the light switch.

One night I gripped the frame of a band room mirror,
stared at my backwater face, a slush of mud and twigs,
my days, a mess of dead fish floating belly-up
and I turned myself away from alcohol,
learned to walk straight
down every street.

I might cut a solo record
with gospel leanings.
The songs would be about gratitude,
all I've survived.

I play chess here in the park.
Each piece has a value and purpose.
Chess asks each player
to consider what they'll
sacrifice and protect.

I make those decisions
every living day.

The tipping point

Marriage counsellor's office.
Two pot plants
in need of water.

Pending their divorce

Now at the supermarket
she buys fewer
of his favourite snacks.

Distribution

Gathered to discuss their father's estate,
Wolfgang offers his two brothers
more cake.

Heated

Conversation at the urinal.
We don't see eye to eye.

Some observations and suggestions

A banana makes a poor crowbar.

The true non-conformist types with their nose.

If you want some heat, try rubbing two sticklers together.

Don't paint yourself into a coroner.

Many long for a whale of a time, while having an ant of a time.

In some nudist colonies, it's a blessing to be short-sighted.

Self-portrait, lying on the bed, Skopelos, 26 September 2018

Let the sea
pound the chest of every cliff,
tug at the hem of each pebbled shore.

Over the balcony railing I've thrown every map
and a guidebook to Naples.
Alternative desires—
to recline, to study the ceiling, write poems on the bedsheets,
have taken hold.

Lacking in orangutans,
Southern Europe makes up for that in olives.

Being horizontal in voluntary ways has little equal.
Let your sandals go off on day trips,
engage in conversation with other sandals.

Island bus ride, Skopelos

Bald is our driver—hopefully not the tyres.
Up and around a sadistic number of hairpin bends. Please
Step on the brakes. Even as a token gesture. Please

Return to steering with both hands. The
Inclination to close one's eyes is more seductive than the coastline.
Descent at last. The fabled beach. It exists. With towel and lotion you
Exit the rear door, check the timetable for the last bus back.

Tourist couple

At the lip of the volcano,
their fierce argument
continues.

Bomb blast

Hospitally.

The end of the season, Skopelos

The tourists have gone—many will arrive home before the volley
of postcards they've mailed to uncle Harry, aunt Gladys.
Taverna tables and chairs are stacked, stored.
Family summer houses which gifted passersby with cooking smells,
the sound of clinked glasses of retsina and ouzo,
are shuttered.

Storm-damaged boats are craned onto the concrete pier.
The months of scraping, re-painting and repair have begun.

In his waterfront studio, Dimitri, seated between an ashtray
and a coffee cup, turns his potter's wheel.
Slowly the serving bowl takes shape out of the pale red clay.

Finding a scrap of paper, Dimitri, sketches the gulls
he'll pattern around the bowl's outer rim—
gulls which he's observed for decades,
scholars of both hemispheres
in search of bountiful destinations.

Portrait of Lester Gambell, musician and songwriter, Milledgeville, Georgia, 10 July 1969

In my neighbourhood
I know all the
front porch sweepers,
iced tea drinkers, rose pruners
and rocking chair philosophers,
who tell me their
bible, railroad and cathouse stories.

They wait for
a cooling breeze,
the arrival of the mailman
or a daughter who's
a damn hard-working nurse
but should visit more.

These Southern men and women,
some who've never
finished elementary school,
been married or travelled in an airplane.
Their voices and manners,
ways of looking at soil and sin,
are there in my blood and songs.

How my father would guide
a mule and plow through a cornfield,
needle and thread through
the torn elbow of a work shirt,
a writhing worm onto a fishhook,
were lessons to me,
how any thorough endeavour
is about making your peace with time.

Listening to the songs and hollers of field hands,
travelling tinsmiths and elixir salesmen,
I learned about the voice—
how it could scale a wall, a mountain,
away from the burdens
of the singer.

Music offered respite.
It was water from a well
and the well's there
beneath our ribcage.

Those songs, their melodies and refrains
I broke apart and reset,
pitched them at beer-tilted audiences.
I pickaxed the earth of barroom pianos
looking for veins of gold.

I tried to leave New Orleans
via my open wrists
but a musician friend found me,
blood unravelling
upon the bathroom floor.

After coming out of hospital,
I caught a Greyhound bus to Memphis,
rented a room
above a secondhand furniture store.

In that room I thought about my Pa,
how one night,
reading *To Kill A Mockingbird* in his armchair,
he had a heart attack.

Again lightning
strikes our family tree.

I want to be its sturdiest branch.
I want to live beyond its tainting reach.

Words and music
chase each other
around a rabbit hole,
scramble across
the roofs of trailer park cabins,
make my fingers search for
a pen,
certain notes on the piano,
a chord sequence on a nearby guitar.
None of my lyrics are
one hundred per cent autobiographical.
There has to be some fabrication in there
as shelter, as shield.
I've travelled far to try to understand
why I've travelled so far
and sometimes I pull my own leg
to get a little further.

My first banjo,
missing two strings,
was instrumental in my defection
away from the mapped and known.

I lit up and out,
a skeleton boy on the open road.

In a Chicago pawnshop
I traded my heart for an anvil
on which I pounded and bent into shape,
an abstract version of myself,
wearing on stage—my battle dress,
made out of hubcaps, chewing gum,
bison teeth and shoeshine rags.
A recording studio is a harbour.

Playing live
you're on the open sea—
there's fear, beauty,
electrical storms.
The band is your crew.
Sometimes there's a mutinous ego,
maybe your own
and you hit a jagged reef,
not the floating riff
you thought you had
at your fingertips.

How many takes it takes
doesn't matter.
The ear's a better listener
than the heart.

Proverbs for the 21st century

People in glass houses shouldn't throw parties.

Never look a gift voucher in the mouth.

Not every clod has a silver lining.

Lunch before you leap.

What's good for the goose, let the goose decide.

Poem for Ed Ruscha

Home on the strange.

It takes two to tangle.

I'll send out a search party animal.

Emotional baggage claim.

Goody three shoes.

You could have knocked me over with a father.

I've grown accustomed to her faeces.

A penitentiary for your thoughts.

Portrait of a hypochondriac

Hips. Heart. Head. Each ache is volcanic. So
Easily and often I feel faint, feverish, nauseous, am
Always misdiagnosed, misunderstood.
Laxatives. Aspirin. Valium. X-rays. Saunas. Supplements.
Transfusions. Each of my organs and orifices
Has a shelf life. I want to marry an ambulance driver.

At my craft

Sometimes I sit at the kitchen table
at 2 in the morning
and have a go at writing a poem.

It's an informal arrangement
with words
and myself,
sometimes in slippers—
together we face the blank page,
approached as one might approach
a friendly-looking dog,
rather than a firing squad.

The idea is to not strain,
to be relaxed but focused,
to remember that language is playful,
each word, phrase, line and image
may be tested, trialled,
at any time discarded—
after all, you're not chiseling
the words directly into marble,
at least, I hope not.

If and when I finish
a first draft of a poem, I ask myself
"What am I trying to say in this poem
and have I said it clearly and strongly?"
If writing any poem becomes a chore,
the arduous push of a no longer attractive boulder,
up an infertile hill,
I become philosophical,
tell myself—
"No writing time is wasted. You've got
to dig through a lot of dirt to get to the gold."

When I'm nearing the completion
of a book's worth of poems,
I print off the poems
and lay them out on the lounge room floor.
This process, this reality,
makes me look at each poem,
reassess them, often revise them.
I want each poem in the envisaged book
to earn their keep,
illuminate the overlooked.

When facing the blank page I have three P's.
Positivity. Practice. Perseverance—

I remind myself that I have a vocabulary,
some life experience,
that it's ok, a possible relief,
to use words in cheeky, madcap ways.
I've taught myself how to write poems
by spending hundreds, now thousands of hours
arranging and rearranging words,
learning their permutations and possibilities,
accept that I will remain an eternal student of language—
the idea of eternity I find appealing,
imagining the number of afternoon naps
I could have.

I continue. Walk through great and lesser-known cities,
along great and lesser-known rivers,
pause to watch a pale red spider, the size of a comma,
climb the bright green of a grass blade.
Bearing witness to the striving of other creatures,
be they salmon or salespersons,
enables me to continue,
to return to the kitchen table
and write poems
which is what I've done
this Saturday, the 25th of March, 2019.

Observations in the year 2019

The pig and the knife will never be friends.

If sardines had elbows, less would fit in each tin.

Portholes like to travel, windows prefer to stay at home.

Adults have their ways, children have their whys.

At any age you may become what doesn't become you.

In no time at all, there may be no time at all.

Portrait of an adulterer

You're getting even in that jacket,
climbing new stairs in that jacket,
not back for the evening in that jacket.

You're on another planet in that jacket,
your ego is the sun you orbit in that jacket.

You're drinking more in that jacket,
you're thinking less in that jacket,
at your least in that jacket.

You're false but not a false alarm in that jacket.

You were once cherished in that jacket,
you'll be buried in that jacket.

Your name will be sobbed in confessions—
You'll become a regrettable mistake
made by numerous when they were weak.

Those who survive you
will putter forward in their rooms and diaries,
traverse the desert of a carpet
towards the chiming of the doorbell,
relieved or dismayed
that it's some stale visitor,
not you, contagious with lust.

Memorandum

Be known by what you achieve not by what you promise.
Promises are weighty. Be open to guidance—
make use of
the world's scientific, historical and moral knowledge.

In library and headline, each arena,
there's the search for the heroic, the admirable,
those who bring curiosity, diligence and humour
to their endeavours,
who inspire, set an example,
give us reason to reassess
our values, our purpose,
how one might move through the world and among people.

Perhaps our greatest contribution is insight,
gained via research, observation, practice and deep thinking.
Let this stand as our process, our wisdom—
to consider the benefits and cost of our actions
as the clock propels each of us towards the finishing line.

Acknowledgements

Some of these poems, or earlier versions of them, have appeared in the following magazines and journals either in print form or online:
Alba (USA), *The Blue Nib* (Ireland), The Canberra Times, *Cordite, Eloquent Orifice, Hoot (*USA), *One Sentence Poems* (USA), *Right Hand Pointing* (USA), *StylusLit, Takahē* (New Zealand).

Thank you to:

Helen Bakowski and Ophelia Bakowski for sharing their love, patience, skills and valued opinions which make my daily and creative life richer.

Marie Saunier, Claude, Fabio and Jules Caldironi, Bruno Doucey, Murielle Szac, Mireille Vignol, Jim Yamouridis, Ilona Bruveris, Madara Gruntmane, Sandra and Adriano Klavins, for their friendship, knowledge, generosity, hospitality, kindness and the loan or rental of their apartments, in France, Greece and Latvia, which enabledme to realise the environments and atmospheres necessary to specific poems in *Wardrobe of Selves*.

Mark Lelliott of NGS Global, for his friendship, generosity, support and annual poetry commissions, in subject matter I may not have addressed without the impetus and challenge each commission provides.

The owners, managers and staff of The Paperback Bookshop, 60 Bourke Street, and The Hill of Content Bookshop, 86 Bourke Street, for their kindness, conversations, generosity of spirit and for continuing to stock, sell and promote my poetry books to the reading public.

Ophelia Bakowski again for the insightful cover photography and design and the author photo. (www.opheliabakowski.com)

I specialize in reading my poetry in private houses, to groups of eight or more anywhere in the world. For further details contact:
pbakowski54@gmail.com
Mobile: +61 (0)406 029 578

Peter Bakowski was born at any early age in Melbourne, Australia, proceeded to crawl to the nearest map of the world. He memorised shipping lanes, the names of capital cities, rivers and mountain ranges, collected bottle tops, bubble-gum cards, Golden Key, Disney and Marvel comics and was taken to his first public library in Walpole Street, Kew, at the age of eight, by his delicatessen-owning father, Richard Bakowski, a pivotal and holy moment that instilled in Peter a love of words, images, faraway places and questing individuals.

Peter's life has been one of extensive and compulsive reading, travelling and imagining and continues to be so, having survived two major heart operations at the Alfred Hospital, Melbourne, one at the age of six and one at the age of thirty-nine.

Peter, accompanied by Helen and often Ophelia Bakowski, has undertaken numerous funded and self-funded residencies, in Rome, Paris, Berlin, Macau, Suzhou (near Shanghai), Labastide Esparbaïrenque (near Carcassonne), Hobart, Greenmount (near Perth, Western Australia), at the Arthur Boyd Estate, Bundanon, New South Wales, and on the Greek island of Skopelos – each residency enabled Peter to write poems which he couldn't have written without the firsthand experience of the residency.

When not travelling, Peter, Helen (a clothes maker), Buzz (a miniature black poodle) and Ophelia (who also has travel and creativity genes) are usually found in their book, records, fabrics and textiles-laden weatherboard house in the Melbourne inner city suburb of Richmond.

2019 Editions

Palace of Memory: An elegy **Paul Hetherington**
Acting Like a Girl **Sandra Renew**
A Coat of Ashes **Jackson**
Summer Haiku **Owen Bullock**
A Common Garment **Anita Patel**
Giant Steps: Fifty poets on the Apollo 11 moon landing **Various**
The Six Senses **Auhtorised Theft**
Wardrobe of Selves **Peter Bakowski**
Breathing in Stormy Seasons **Stephanie Green**
Strange Creatures **Alyson Miller**

2018 Editions

The Uncommon Feast **Eileen Chong**
Inlandia **KA Nelson**
Peripheral Vision **Martin Dolan**
The Love of the Sun **Matt Hetherington**
Moving Targets **Jen Webb**
Things I Have Thought to Tell You Since I Saw You Last **Penelope Layland**
The Many Uses of Mint **Ravi Shankar**
Abstractions **Various**
ACE: Arresting, Contemporary stories by Emerging Writers **Various**

all titles available from
www.recentworkpress.com

www.ingramcontent.com/pod-product-compliance
Lightning Source LLC
Chambersburg PA
CBHW032050290426
44110CB00012B/1028